USING MAPS

Where we live

by Susan Hoe

ticktock

By Susan Hoe
Series consultant: Debra Voege
Editor: Mark Sachner
Project manager: Joe Harris
***ticktock* designer: Hayley Terry**
Picture research: Lizzie Knowles and Joe Harris

Copyright © 2008 ticktock Entertainment Ltd. First published in Great Britain by ticktock Media Ltd.,
Unit 2, Orchard Business Centre, North Farm Road, Tunbridge Wells, Kent TN2 3XF, Great Britain.

A CIP catalogue record for this book is available from the British Library.

ISBN 978 1 84696 722 1

Printed in China

PICTURE CREDITS

Bananastock: 17tr. Corbis: 21b. Cultura Limited/ SuperStock: 6t. Digital Vision Ltd/ SuperStock: 12br. Chris
George/ Alamy: 19b. Getmapping PLC: 24c. Image100/ SuperStock: 7b. Images of Birmingham/ Alamy: 10b.
iStock: 10t, 17bl, 17br, 22t, 25b. Justin Kase zthreez / Alamy: 15bl. Ulli Seer/ Getty Images: 5t. Shutterstock: 1,
4t, 4b, 6b, 8, 17tl, 20, 24t, 24b, 25t, 25c, 27 all. Justin Spain: 22b, 23. Hayley Terry: 5b, 6b (map), 11t, 11b,
12b, 13, 15br, 31t. Tim Thirlaway: 28, 29. ticktock Media Archive: 30b. Brett Walker: 9 x 4. www.mapart.co.uk:
7t, 14, 15t, 16, 18, 19t, 26, 31b.

Contents

Words in **bold** are explained in the glossary.

What is a map?

A map is a special drawing. This drawing is usually of an area as seen from above.

This area can be as big as a whole country. Or it can be as small as your bedroom!

Making a map of an island

Map Key

 Trees/woods

 Roads/footpaths

Grey-roofed buildings

Red-roofed buildings

 Pier

 Gardens

Maps help us find things as if we were directly above them.

In this book, we are going to see how maps show us about the places where people live. But first let's look at some of the ways that maps can help us.

Find the longest pier in the photo of the island.

Now find it on the map.

Why do we need maps?

Maps help us find our way around. They give us all kinds of information about where we live.

A map can help you get from one place to another. It can show you where you are, where you want to go and how to get there.

Weather map of the UK and Ireland

This map shows you what the weather will be like where you live.

Can you tell what kinds of weather this map is showing?

World Map

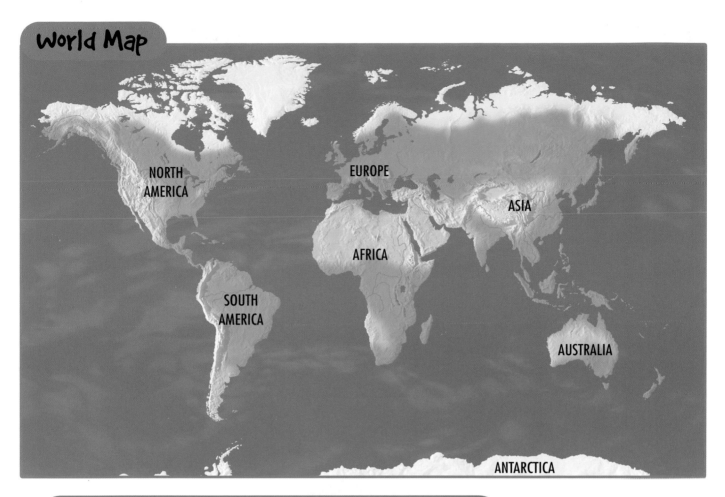

This map shows the world's deserts in yellow. The forests and woods are in green. Places covered in snow and ice are white.

Maps teach us important facts about places. These places might be close to home or on the other side of the world.

Maps can show us whether the land is flat or hilly. They also show us where people and animals live. We can also learn what **crops** are grown and what sorts of things are made in a place.

Maps are handy and easy to use. They can show us huge areas in a small amount of space. We can take them just about anywhere!

Mapping your bedroom

Maps show how a place looks if you are looking down on it. That place can be a country or a town. It can even be your bedroom!

A 3-D room

This room is a **three-dimensional (3-D)** space. The room and the things in the room are solid. They have length, width, and **depth**.

A 2-D map

A map is a flat, **two-dimensional (2-D)** drawing of a space. In a map, all the objects look flat. They have only length and width.

To create a 2-D map of this bedroom, we draw all the flat shapes on a piece of paper.

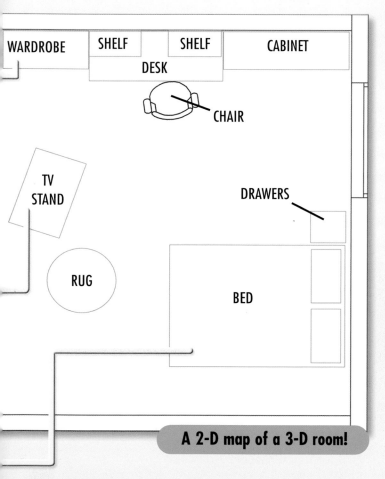

WARDROBE SHELF SHELF CABINET

DESK

CHAIR

TV STAND

DRAWERS

RUG

BED

A 2-D map of a 3-D room!

This map shows you the room and everything in it.

Find the rug.   **Find the chair.**

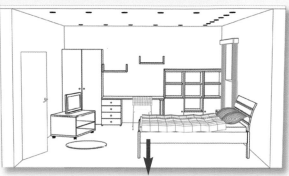

This drawing of the room was made from the photograph.

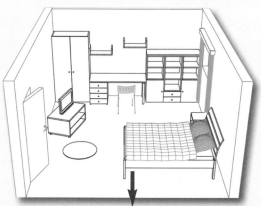

Pretend you are able to float up above the room and look down on it.

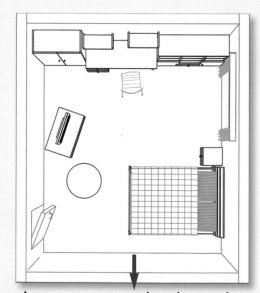

When you are right above the room, it looks flat. This is the view we use to make a 2-D map.

Mapping your town

We've made a map of a room, but you can also use maps to show larger areas. When you look at a map of your town, you can see all the interesting places. You can also figure out how to find them.

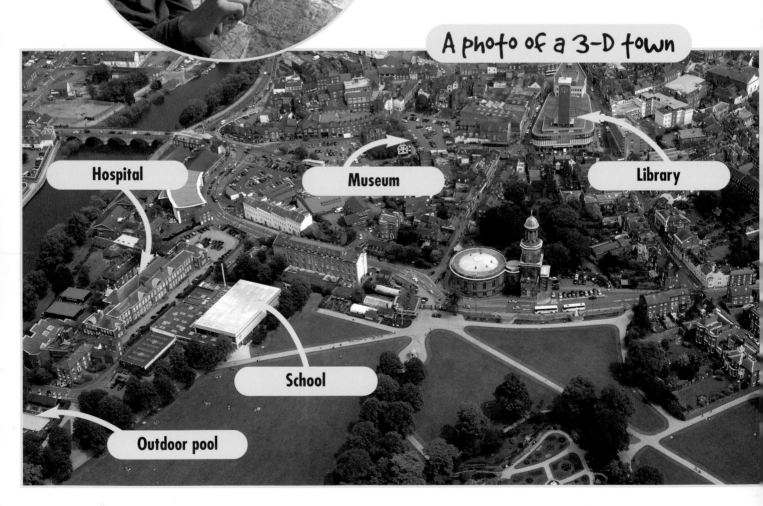

A photo of a 3-D town

Hospital

Museum

Library

School

Outdoor pool

This photo shows many interesting places in a town. They are in the photo, but they might be hard to find without a map to identify them.

A 2-D map of the town

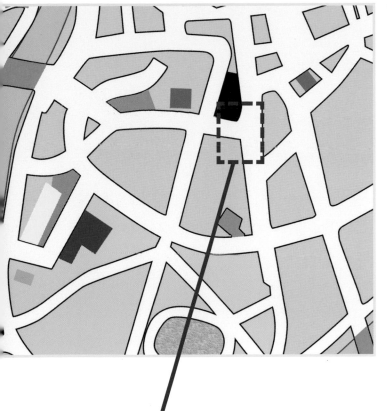

This map shows where the important places are located. It uses different **symbols** to identify each place. The map has a key. This **map key** is also called a legend. It tells you what each symbol stands for.

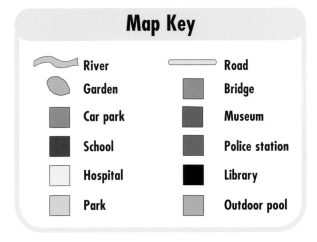

Map Key

~	River	—	Road
	Garden		Bridge
	Car park		Museum
	School		Police station
	Hospital		Library
	Park		Outdoor pool

This map shows more details about your town. The symbols and the map key make it easy to show lots of things on the map – and they are easy to read!

Map Key

	Streetlight
	Postbox
	Rubbish bin
	Trees/shrubs
	Bench
	Road

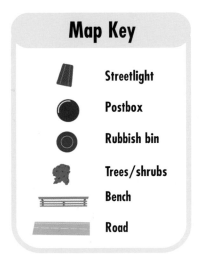

Where are the rubbish bins in this street?

Using your town map

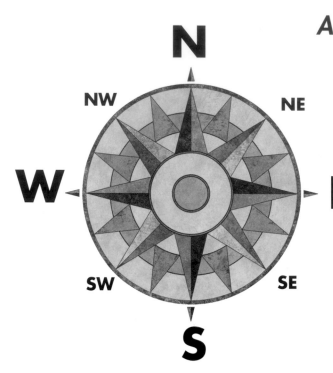

A map usually has a compass guide. The guide points to the four main directions on the map – north (N), south (S), east (E), and west (W). The compass guide shown here is called a compass rose.

A **compass rose** may also show northeast (NE), southeast (SE), southwest (SW), and northwest (NW). These are found in between north, south, east and west.

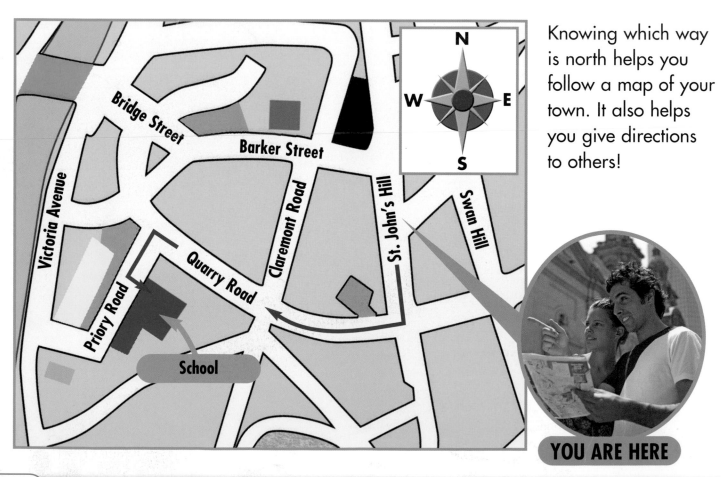

Knowing which way is north helps you follow a map of your town. It also helps you give directions to others!

YOU ARE HERE

Buildings in your town

Buildings are often placed along major roads. In this way, most people can get to them easily.

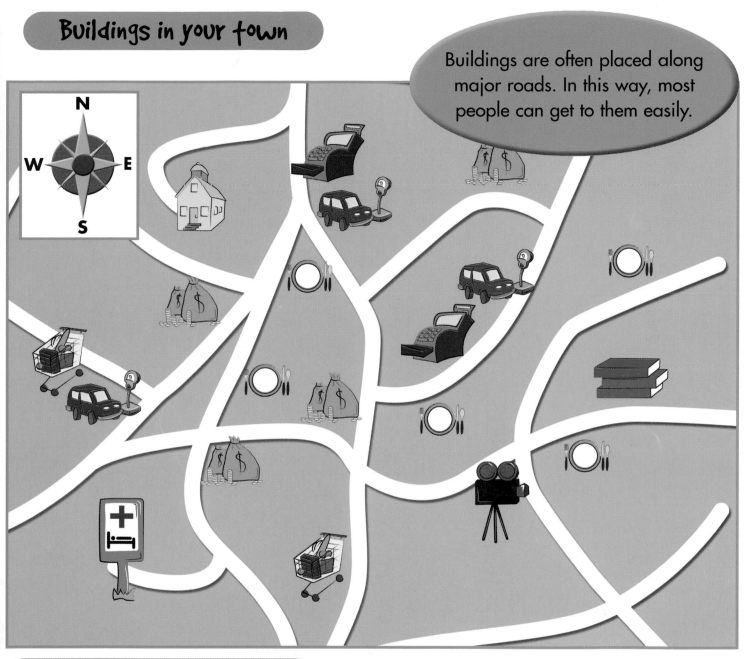

Map Key

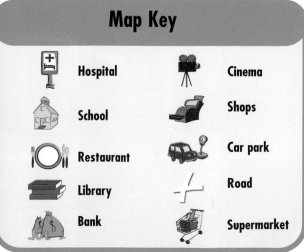

Hospital		Cinema	
School		Shops	
Restaurant		Car park	
Library		Road	
Bank		Supermarket	

Here are some buildings found in a town: supermarkets, restaurants, libraries, hospitals, cinemas, banks, and shops. Most schools and shops are built where people live – in their neighbourhoods.

Find the supermarkets and the school.

Mapping your country

You can show more than one town on a map. In fact you can show your whole country! To show a very large area, like the United Kingdom, the area must be drawn smaller, or scaled down, to fit on a piece of paper. The map will show lots of area, but not many details.

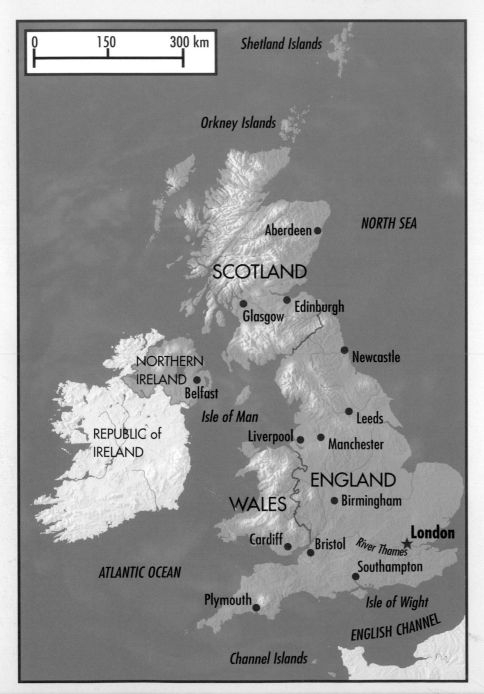

| 0 | 150 | 300 km |

Shetland Islands

Orkney Islands

NORTH SEA

Aberdeen •

SCOTLAND

Glasgow • • Edinburgh

NORTHERN
IRELAND •
  Belfast

Newcastle •

Isle of Man

Liverpool • Leeds •

REPUBLIC of
IRELAND

 • Manchester

ENGLAND

WALES   • Birmingham

Cardiff • Bristol • River Thames ★ London

ATLANTIC OCEAN

Southampton •

Plymouth •

Isle of Wight

ENGLISH CHANNEL

Channel Islands

The **scale** on this map of the United Kingdom is very small. Only a few details are shown.

Map Key

★ Capital city

● City

14

This map of the Isle of Wight has a larger scale. More details are on this map. You can see many cities, and land features, such as major rivers.

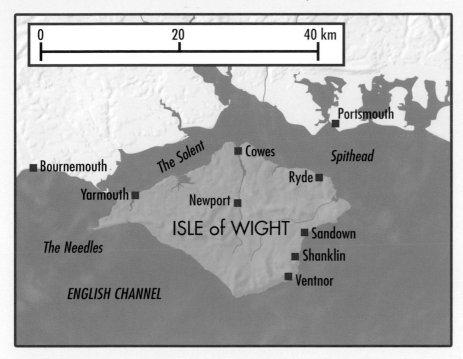

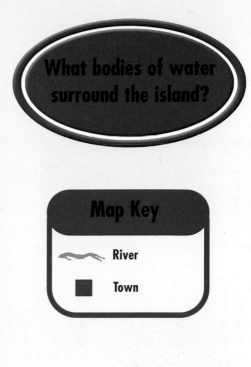

What bodies of water surround the island?

Map Key

～～～ River

■ Town

Towns and water routes

Many towns were first built next to rivers, lakes, and oceans.

With a **water route** nearby, ships could move goods from place to place. People could also travel more easily. Today, many of those towns have grown to become major cities, like London (shown below).

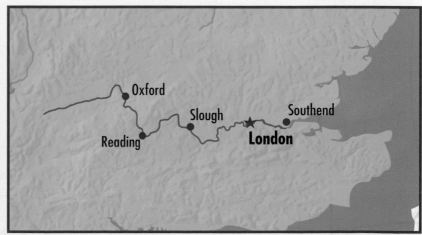

This map shows the winding River Thames. It also shows the towns that grew along its banks.

Mapping the world

The United Kingdom is part of Europe, which is a large area of land called a **continent**. There are seven continents on maps of the world: North America, South America, Africa, Europe, Asia, Australia, and Antarctica.

Maps come in two forms: **physical maps** and **political maps**.

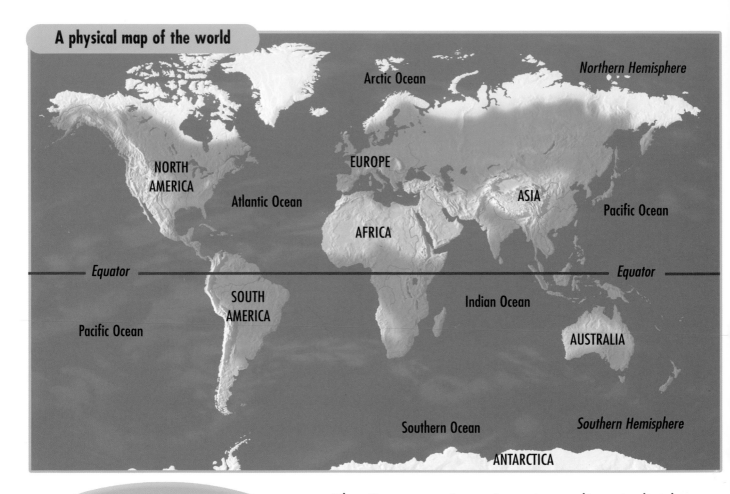

A physical map of the world

Northern Hemisphere

Arctic Ocean

NORTH AMERICA

EUROPE

ASIA

Pacific Ocean

Atlantic Ocean

AFRICA

Equator

Equator

SOUTH AMERICA

Indian Ocean

Pacific Ocean

AUSTRALIA

Southern Ocean

Southern Hemisphere

ANTARCTICA

A physical map shows the natural features of the continents. These include bodies of water, mountains, forests, and deserts.

The **Equator** is an imaginary line. It divides Earth into two halves. One half is the Northern Hemisphere. The other half is the Southern Hemisphere. Europe is north of the Equator.

one continent, many countries

A political map shows how continents are divided into countries. People who live in the same continent often speak different languages.

A political map of Europe

In Spain, most people speak Spanish.

In the United Kingdom, most people speak English.

A political map of Africa

Ghana

Kenya

The official languages in Kenya are Swahili and English.

Most people in Ghana speak English.

What would it be like to live in an African country? Let's find out!

Mapping a country in Africa: Sudan

A physical map of Africa

Africa is a large continent. It has more than fifty countries. It also has many natural features.

The map key shows that Africa has large dry deserts, rainforest jungles, grasslands and mountains. Africa also has four main rivers. They are the Nile, Congo, Niger, and Zambezi.

SAHARA DESERT

Nile River

Niger River

SUDAN

Congo River

Zambezi River

Map Key

	Grasslands
	Desert
	Rainforest
	Mountains
	River/lake

Sudan is the largest country in Africa. Its land features range from dry deserts and grasslands to mountainous areas (shown in tan). The Blue Nile and the White Nile rivers meet at Khartoum. Here, they form the mighty Nile River.

Find Khartoum, the capital city of Sudan, on the map.

A physical map of Sudan

LIBYA

EGYPT

Red Sea

Nubian Desert

Port Sudan

Nile River

CHAD

Omdurman

★ Khartoum

Blue Nile

SUDAN

White Nile

ETHIOPIA

CENTRAL AFRICAN REPUBLIC

▲ Mt. Kinyet

A world apart

Sudan and the United Kingdom are located on different continents, thousands of kilometres apart. Sudan is mostly flat and has dry deserts, while the United Kingdom is covered with hills and low-lying grassy fields.

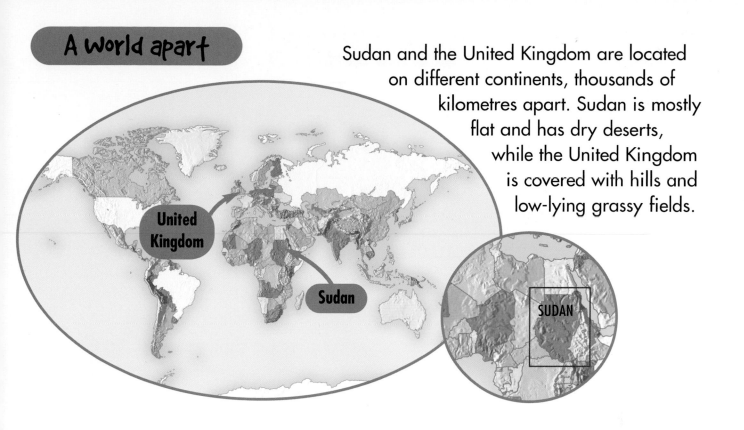

Desert makes up much more of the land in Sudan. This is why the most important towns in Sudan, like Khartoum (below), grew up along the banks of rivers.

The Blue Nile flows through Khartoum.

Mapping Grace's village

This is Grace's village in Sudan, Africa. Fifty people live in the village. Instead of wood or brick houses like those found in the United Kingdom, the villagers live in big huts called **tukuls**.

The homes in Grace's village do not have running water. So Grace has an important job to do. She must collect water from the well for her family every morning.

The people in Grace's village grow their fruits and vegetables in nearby gardens. They grow pumpkins, tomatoes, maize, and a type of grain called sorghum. They raise goats in pens for milk and meat.

Grace's Village

The map of Grace's village uses symbols to represent different parts of its community. The map key helps you understand what the symbols stand for.

Map Key

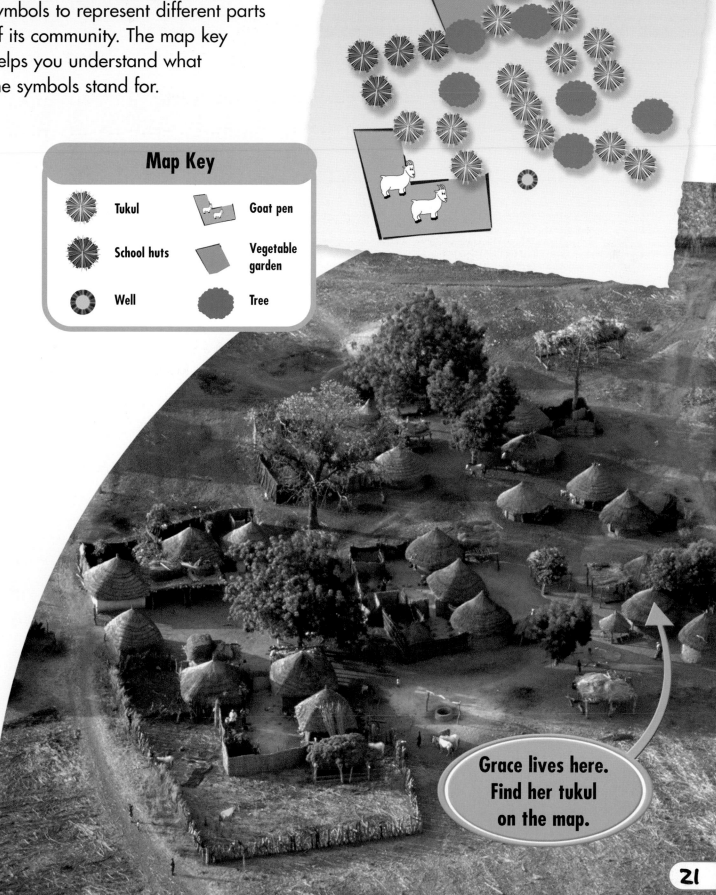 Tukul		Goat pen	
School huts		Vegetable garden	
Well		Tree	

Grace lives here. Find her tukul on the map.

Drawing maps

Before you can draw a map, you must figure out the exact size and shape of the mapping area. This means figuring out how to measure large areas.

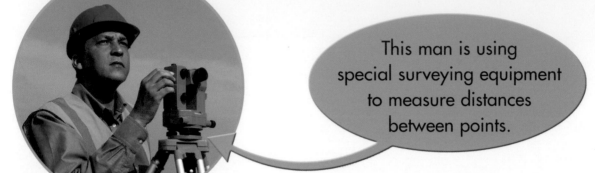

This man is using special surveying equipment to measure distances between points.

Mapmakers use their measurements to draw their maps. The maps on these pages show the attractions at an amusement park.

Scale: shrinking to fit

When mapmakers have gathered all their measurements, they must figure out how to fit them onto a piece of paper. So they shrink, or scale down, the real measurements to make a map.

0   15 metres

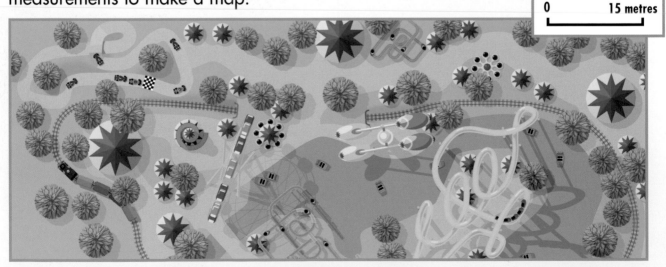

This small-scaled map shows a fairly large area. Many objects are visible, but they are quite small.

Different scales used to map the same area change what you see. Small-scale maps show large areas on a sheet of paper. Large-scale maps show smaller areas, but the objects look bigger and have more detail.

The map scale tells you how long a metre is on the map. This way you can figure out real distances on the map.

0   8 metres

This larger-scaled map shows a smaller area than the first map. The map scale also shows that each centimetre is equal to fewer metres. So you see fewer objects on this map, but you can see them in greater detail.

0   5 metres

This map has the largest scale. It shows an even smaller area. You see even fewer objects, but you can see them in even greater detail.

Hi-tech mapmaking

*Many years ago, people used their travels to figure out the shape of the land. Today, mapmakers use new, **hi-tech** equipment.*

Mapmakers can take many photographs of the ground from a plane.

This photograph shows the ground below as seen from the plane.

The pictures and measurements taken from the plane are sent to computers that draw a map.

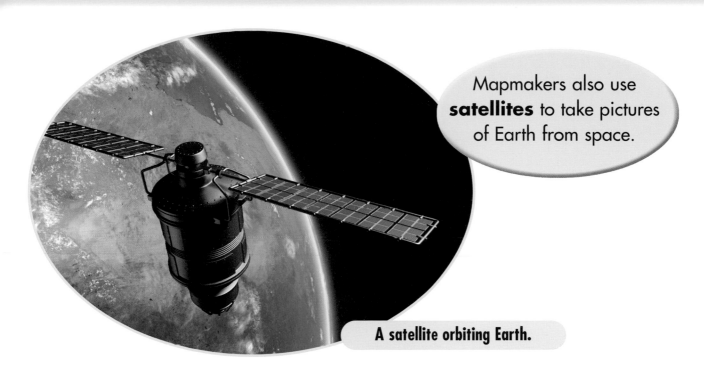

Mapmakers also use **satellites** to take pictures of Earth from space.

A satellite orbiting Earth.

The pictures taken by these satellites are beamed back to Earth. They are put together to make pictures of our planet, like the one shown here. These pictures can then be turned into maps.

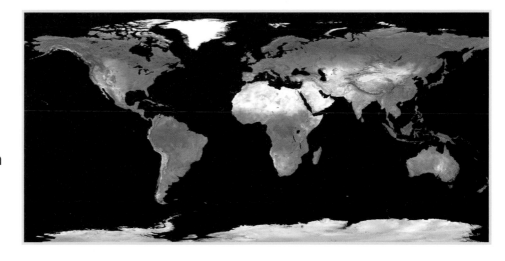

Ever-Changing maps

Satellites can tell where your car is on the road. They can produce road maps that help you find your destination. These maps constantly change as you need them. The maps are called **GPS**, or Global Positioning System, maps.

A GPS map at work in a car.

Mapping African animals

Africa is home to thousands of different kinds of animals. Some live in jungles. Some live on grassy plains. Others live in rivers. Here's how you can create a map that shows where they live!

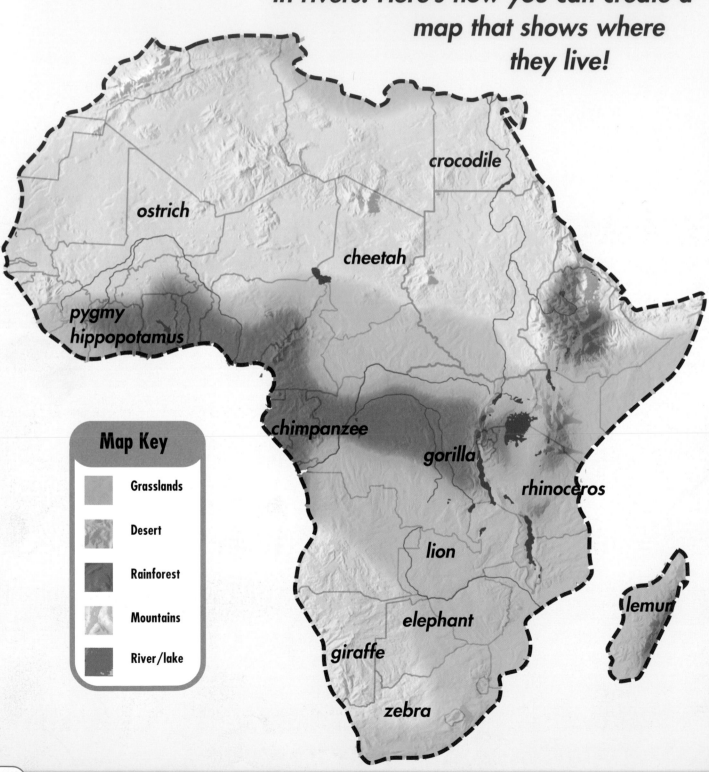

Map Key

Grasslands

Desert

Rainforest

Mountains

River/lake

crocodile

ostrich

cheetah

pygmy hippopotamus

chimpanzee

gorilla

rhinoceros

lion

elephant

lemur

giraffe

zebra

How to make a map of the animals of Africa

1 Copy the map of Africa on page 26 onto a blank sheet of paper. You can also use a thin piece of tracing paper to trace the map.

2 Now make an animal map key. Draw pictures on it of the animals shown below.

3 The map on page 26 shows where each animal lives. Use this map as a guide to draw your own animal pictures on your map of Africa. Be sure to draw the animals so they look like the ones in your animal map key. You have now made a map of where African animals live.

Animal Map Key

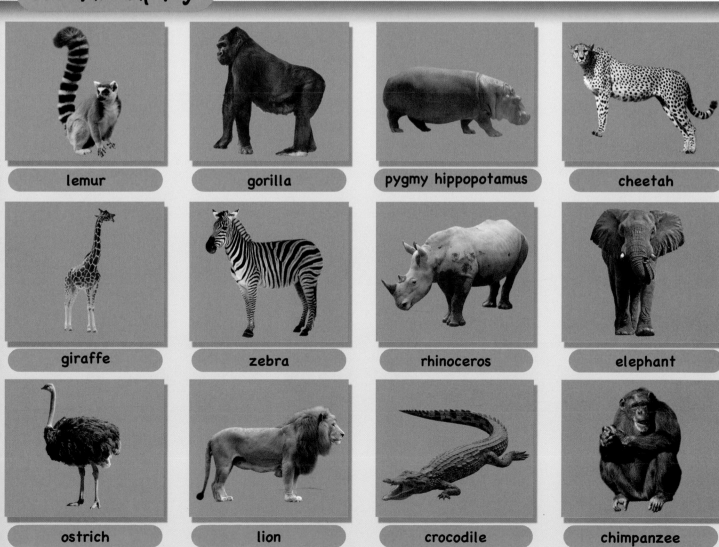

lemur	gorilla	pygmy hippopotamus	cheetah
giraffe	zebra	rhinoceros	elephant
ostrich	lion	crocodile	chimpanzee

Making a playground map

Playgrounds are fun places to visit. Make a map of your dream playground. Include all of your favourite playground activities! Make a map key so your friends can find all the great things in your playground map.

What is the shape of your playground? Round, square, rectangular, oval?

What kinds of plants are on your playground? Trees, flowers, bushes?

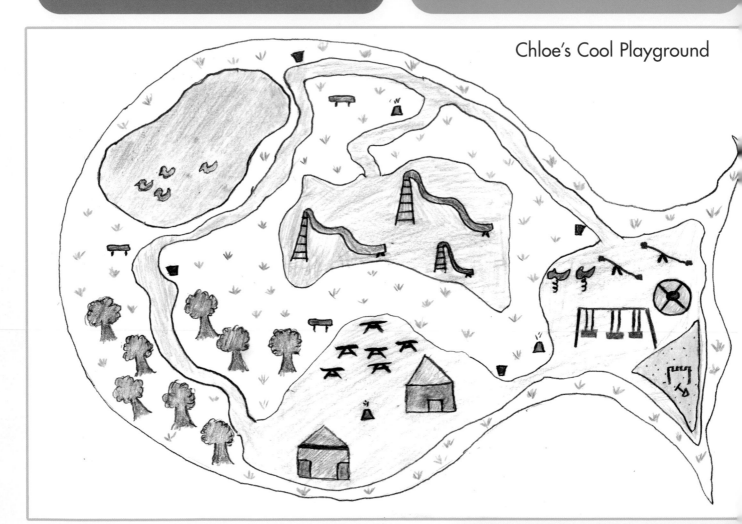

Chloe's Cool Playground

What kinds of rides and activities does your playground have? Swings, slides, roundabouts, rocking animals, a climbing frame, a sandpit?

Step 1

Draw the shape of your playground on a piece of paper.

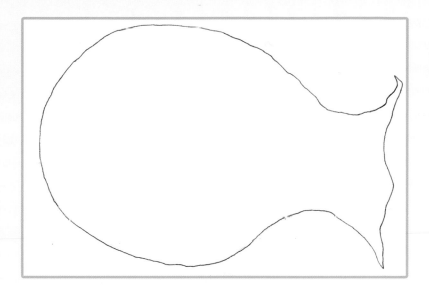

Step 2

Make up different symbols for all the playground items you want to include on your map. Be sure you leave enough space between all the different symbols. Draw in paths and grassy areas too.

Step 3

Colour your playground map and give it a name.

Step 4

Make your map key using the symbols on your map.

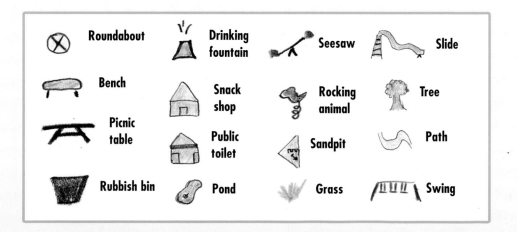

Roundabout
Drinking fountain
Seesaw
Slide
Bench
Snack shop
Rocking animal
Tree
Picnic table
Public toilet
Sandpit
Path
Rubbish bin
Pond
Grass
Swing

Glossary

Compass rose: a drawing that shows directions on a map: north (N), south (S), east (E) and west (W).

Continent: a large body of land. There are seven continents on Earth.

Crops: plants that are grown for food or other purposes. Fruits, vegetables, grains, and nuts are crops.

Depth: the length from the top of a space or object, to its bottom.

Equator: an imaginary line that circles Earth halfway between the North and South poles. The top half is the Northern Hemisphere. The bottom half is the Southern Hemisphere.

GPS (global positioning system): an instrument that uses satellites to show drivers how to get to a place. As the car is moving, the instrument shows the driver directions on a screen.

Hi-tech (high-technology): coming from the newest forms of science and technology.

Map key: the space on a map that shows the meaning of any pictures or colours used on the map.

Physical maps: maps that show rivers, oceans, mountains and other land features.

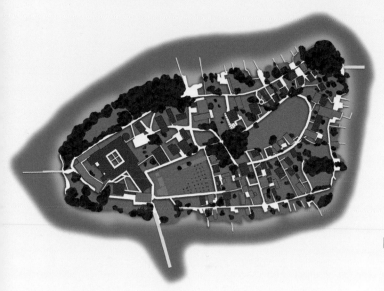

Three-dimensional (3-D): appearing as a solid thing that has length, width, and depth.

Tukuls: huts found in parts of Africa. The walls are made of mud. The cone-shaped roofs are made of straw.

Two-dimensional (2-D): appearing as a flat shape with only length and width.

Political maps: maps that show countries or states. Borders outline each area.

Satellite: an object launched by a rocket that circles and studies Earth or other bodies in space. It then sends information back to Earth.

Water route: a way to get people and goods from one place to another by boat or ship. The water route can be a river, stream or open ocean.

Scale: the amount by which the measurement of an area is shrunk to fit on a map. The map scale is a drawing or symbol that tells how to measure distances on a map.

Symbols: pictures or drawings that stand for different things on a map.

Index